Unfinished: Elements & Dragons

Unfinished: Elements & Dragons

Ashley Heffner

Contents

1

When the sun falls

When the sun finally falls,
And the trees lose their voice,
Letting darkness make a home,
I will sit with you in silence.

2

A wish

I wish I could teach you to be brave,
But I can show you strength,
And love.

3

Elements & Dragons

Roller coaster : Life
Demons : Fears
Fight : Control
Chaos : Order
My sweet boy calls it Elements and Dragons.

4

Humble

Take the loss.
Do not let your anger defeat you.
Humble yourself.
Take the loss.

5

Anxiety

What if?....
What may?....
What will?....
What could?....
What would?...
Sincerely,
Anxiety.

6

Glow

Be the glimmer,
The night light,
The subtle light lurking in the shadows,
I never wanted to be the brightest,
I wanted to glow.

7

Value

I love to remember how valueless perfection is,
And how invaluable all our quirks and faults are,
We should value ourselves more.

8

Myself

I keep falling,
Remolding,
Loosing pieces
Rebuilding,
And
Experiencing my own art.

9

My soul

To the boy with the wild hair
And the girl who carries fire,
I love you over the moon,
And throughout the galaxies.

10

Lost Dream

Am I the shooting star,
The aftermath,
A glimmer of hope,
Or the lost dream?

11

Sensitive & Graceful

I'm sensitive,
You judge me as overly emotional,
Weak and aloof.
Your misjudgments are what blinds you,
What keeps you from seeing my strengths,
My courage and my grace.

12

Panick attacks

Skin vibrating,
Breathless,
Void words,
Muffled noise,
Spinning,
Exploding chest,
Heavy hands,
Numb,
Dark,
Panick attacks.

13

Butter People

Some people are like butter,
If you try to soften them to quickly,
They will melt and fall apart,
Let them sit and rest,
They will soften at their own pace,
Be patient and wait,
They always make the best cookies.
All my love,
The weird girl.

14

Crumbling

I want to cry,
scream,
cry some more,
and just go to sleep.
My body wants to give up,
and my mind is constant,
but I cant cry,
I cant scream,
and I cant sleep.
So much panick,
and fear of everything falling apart,
my anxieties keep me awake at night,
and a prisoner,
to all the what ifs that will never come to light.
I just want to intake a full breath of air,
without feeling like I will crumble on the exhale.

15

Childhood

Bright red sweaty little faces,
High pitched belly laughs,
Tiny dirty hands,
Scraped knees,
And a forest,
Full of imagination,
Sticks are no longer sticks,
They're immaculate swords,
And staffs,
The acorns turn to gold coins,
The dandelion wishes have faces,
And the fallen leaves become great feasts.

16

Rainboots

I don't know what I am doing,
Just planning,
And hoping it don't all go sideways,
But sometimes,
The rain is nice,
And unexpected blooms are worth it,
So I wear my rainboots.

17

Stuck

Being motivated,
And unmotivated,
All at the same time,
Is such a stuck feeling,
My brain never shuts off,
And my body just wants to give up.

18

Planted

I like flowers better when,
They are planted,
I love watching the moon,
And counting the stars,
Crunchy leaves next to a fire,
Dark rooms,
Music,
Weird makeup,
Black birds,
Tarot,
Tea over coffee,
And comfy clothes.

19

Overthinking

Always,
Radiating anxiety,
And impressively,
Overthinking.

20

Goodnight

Goodnight,
With a kiss on your head,
And a hug to keep you warm,
Goodnight,
With a giggle,
And Eskimo kisses.